Reader Advice:

LIFE

Life is,
Not what you take of it

Life is,
What you make of it!

Living
Poems for an Awesome! Life

Sunrise

Early morning hours, the sky turns 100 colors
In shades of blue, purple, orange and red
The peaceful easiness that is inspired
While the rest of the world is still in bed

No noise, only nature in the wee morning light
Just peace, calm and gentleness..the world seems just right

Anything is possible on the days that you can early wake,
Seems there are no troubles, nor troubles can they make

Ah, to enjoy the early morning sunrise
Where you and nature can be one
If only I can get my butt out of bed
So I can actually see one!

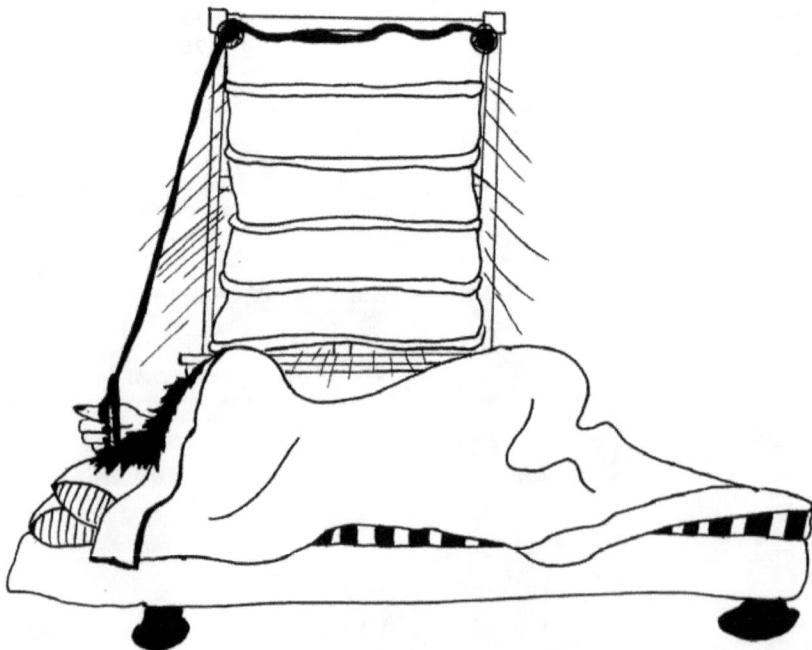

Wake Up!

ARRRGGGHHH!

I want a ...

*Remote control snooze button, complete with automatic
smack switch, triple powered battery and solar backup, pin-
point accuracy, works perfect in long and short distances,
finger or fist activated, non-intrusive manual and/or mental
control, refillable morning water purifier with lemon-fla-
vored instamatic eye-opener and fueled with optimism that
inspires creativity, effectiveness and instills an overall
feeling of:*
AWESOME!

This is all I want, all I need
Because waking up early is just no fun!
Do you know where I can find one?

*For the optimal reading experience
Here's a plan:
Read the *part* as fast as you can

How Ya Feelin'?

When you Feel down ,,, get UP!

When you Feel low ,,, think HIGH!

When you Feel sad ,,, find GLAD!

When you Feel broken ,,, be WHOLE!

When you Feel alone ,,, feel TOGETHERNESS!

Afraid to begin? ... be BRAVE and START!

Goin' short? Go LONG!

Start Small ... Dream BIG ... FINISH STRONG!

Mirror Mirror

There is a wonderful women that lives behind my mirror

She tells me how handsome I am

Every morning I jump out of bed

I just can't wait to see 'er

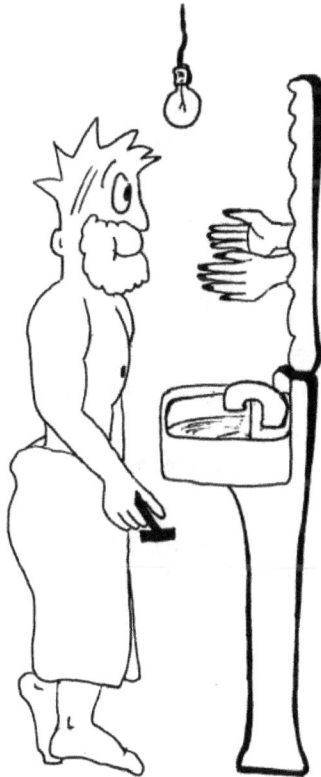

My Dreams First!

Why don't we remember our silliest dreams?
Probably, we would spend all day thinking about them
And what they all mean

Like: Why is the purple polka dotted elephant standing on
one leg serving chicken-wing ice cream
at the Martian elementary school for acrobats?
Or...Why the pizza-flavored gelato mountaintop people are `
running out of chopsticks and have to use lollipop handles
to pole-vault over the bare-naked bookworms?

It might take all day to discover
What's the scheme to our dreams
We would be so caught up in deciphering
It would leave no time to cook and clean

We would forget our duties and overlook our chores
No time for yard work, no textbooks
Nor grocery shopping in stores

The entire society just might collapse I am told
If we had to unveil just how our dreams unfold

The whole dang system just might shut down
If everyone tried it at the same time
Hmmmm, better you go on with your work
And I'll just start figuring out mine!

Flying High

While flying through the sky, higher than high
In a miraculous airborne machine
I could not help to wonder
How I've overlooked in the past
The beauty of travelling so high and so fast
Risin' and risin'
Over the horizon

How have I overlooked the glory of flying?
Of soaring like a bird through the air?
How is this not amazing, not wondrous not thrilling?
It's tremendous! It's Awesome! It's...

Excuse me, What did you say?
Close the window shade for you?
The movie is starting on channel 2?
It's the premiere debut?
Of a vampire superhero robot soccer player
Whose skin is colored blue?
Yes, I'm sorry for the glare
You caught me in mid-stare
There...the shade is down
Your screen is bright
Now, is everything in YOUR world all right?
Your video is streaming
So, if you'll excuse me
I am going back to my daydreaming

New Holiday!

I would like to announce a new holiday
It's something that we must now declare
Every year and everyone will have a day
Where they can work at home in their underwear!

We already have holidays where we close banks
And we give Thanks
There are holidays for wars, deaths and Gods
We have holidays for Presidents and Kings
Bunnies and even groundhogs!

So, why not a holiday
Where the day is free to choose
Where it's completely free of obligations
And you have absolutely nothing to lose?

You may spend it with a friend
Or find some time alone
Spend it reading a book
Or catching up on the telephone

Spend it how you want
It's totally up to you I swear
Just remember, however you spend it
Promise me...
That you'll be in your underwear

3 AM

I woke up at 3 AM (in the morning)...
In the middle of the night

It sounded like angels were calling my name!
So, I got up and looked for the reason...
Like it was a scavenger hunt sorta game

I turned off the two open faucets
That were pouring out hot water
I put away the knives drying (points up) in the kitchen,
Just like they say that you oughter

I closed the open windows right before the big rain
And I moved my car off the railroad tracks,
To not disturb the morning train

And after a few hours,
I never did seem to find out
What the angels where yelling about

Pobre Feeto

While putting on my socks today
I became strangely aware
.....that my feet would enjoy no light this day
Nor breathe any cool fresh air

While my hands go free and my mouth runs dry
My feet are all socked and shoed
....And I think my feet are grand
Imagine if I didn't like them...
What worse could I do?

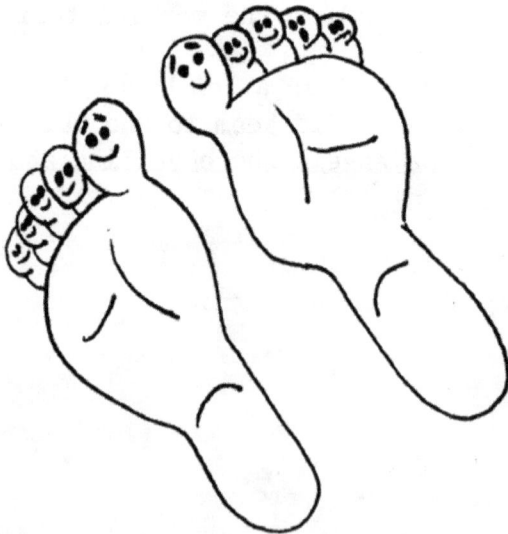

Beep!

Checked into the hospital for some much needed rest...
That is what they said is best

They hooked me up to monitors
And I laid right down for some sleep
After five minutes...Beep!

Time for a test
Another five minutes
Rest.....Beep!

Time for a meal
Rest....Beep!
How do you feel?
Rest..... Beep!

Do you need anything?
Rest..... Beep!
If you need anything please ring
Rest...Beep!
All these machines are driving me mad,
I can't rest a peep!
BEEP!!

I think I will check in to my home for some sleep!!
BEEP!!!

Not A 'ting

My brother is 18
My sister's age is 20
Grandma says she's 12
I think that's kind of funny

My Dad says he's 40
And I am 27
My neighbor is 22
And my best friend acts 11

Some people like their ages
For some, it makes them feel glummer...
To me, you are only as old as you feel
So, why worry about the number?

'illions

I've told you a hundred thousand million billion
trillion quadrillion quintillion sextillion septillion
octillion nonillion decillion undecillion duodecillion
tredecillion quattuordecillion quindecillian sexdecillion
septendecillion octodecillion novemdecillion vigintillion
times -

Don't

EXAGGERATE!!!!!!

This Dog!

I've gotta walk the dog
In the fog …
And In the snow!
Until he decides to go

I've gotta walk the dog
It's such a drag on days like this
I'd rather be in my bed
Although my dog has to...go

I've gotta walk the dog
And it's negative degrees!
He just can't cross his legs all day
And he's shaking at the knees!

I've gotta walk the dog

Even though he's so small and I am large
Sometimes I wonder just who's in charge?

Stick With It!

We gave it our best
We put ourselves through the test

We gave it all we had
Mostly Awesome, some... not too bad

We left the tank dry
We did better than "try"

We pushed mind, body and spirit to the limit
To help our team win it

Were we perfect? "No"
I'm not worried though

Did we make mistakes?
Sure...nevertheless we didn't break

Our team stood strong
Like we have all along

Let us never quit
We are too Awesome to do it

Let's stay together and you will see
The Best is Yet to Be

St'Opera

While talking to her, it's as clear as can be
All she wanted to do was talk about "me"
Just not "me" as in "me"
I mean "me" as in "she"
And not even a "we"
Just me me me me!
Like Luciano Pavarotti

Singing me Me ME ME!

I start talking of news...she says
'Well, let me tell you about me'
I change to discussing my day, she says
'Wait till you hear about me'
All my wins big and small, pale in comparison to she

Seems like a curse, however, things could be worse
What she needs me for is to listen
To verse after verse
About all the things in her life
And how they all work

The silent listener for her stories
I should be "proud that she chose me"
At least that's what she tells me
That's the line that she sells me

So, I guess that's my unofficial profession
To listen to her endless confessions
About her new and daily obsessions

And who am I to disagree?
Well, I earned an honorary degree
A Masters High-Honor Doctorate Ph.D
In "talking" about "me"

Rubber-Necking

The traffic is jammed, and what's the reason?
Ah, maybe it's a parade! NO, it's just not the season

Perhaps an oil spill
Or maybe, busted boulders on the highway
I'd have someone clean it up fast
If I could always have my way

Ah! It must be a car wreck,
I hope no one is hurt
Or maybe, it's a UFO coming to talk to those of us on Earth

No one knows why the rubberneckers stop to look and listen
No one knows why the cars grind to a crawl
Everyone is very interested in the scene
Even though there is nothing to see at all

Yes, the delay is for nothing
There's no reason to bother
The two lanes of traffic slowed down it seems
Just to look at each other!

Bed Head

Why do people choose a side of the bed?
Yes, they choose a side of the bed to reside

The left or the right, they can argue all night
About what's the bed's best side to be shut-eyed

For me, the few sides I have tried
The left and the right,
The head and the foot, and the middle
Seem all very common. Yes, all very boring
So, I choose not to argue or quibble

The bed's best side, may be the untried
That's right
The best side of the bed, is the one left unsaid

So, if you have to decide
Then like me, say with pride…
"I prefer to sleep on the underside!"

Balance

For every up
There may be a down
For every smile
There may be a frown

For every Yang
There's a Yin
There's a balance
In everything

For every child laughing
There may be another one crying
However, that does NOT mean
You should ever stop trying

You must keep moving on
You must keep pushing through
You must keep on winning
And You must keep True to You!

In the end,
There's only one sure way to measure it:
Did you find your life's True Passion?
And Do You TREASURE it?

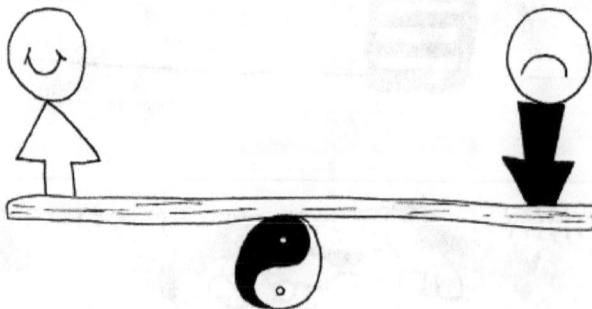

Constellations

The stars while in flight
Are an incredible sight

The ancients had it right
When they all came out at night
And dreamed up the pictures in the sky so bright

For with today's city lights
Even when we try with all our might
We can see only a few stars twinkling white

From Rome to Babylonia
From China to Macedonia
From Polynesia to Patagonia

People imagined patterns of great celestial scenes
Those days were full of wonder and dreams
Now all people do is...stare at video screens:(

BF's

Everyone needs a best friend
A real best friend
Someone you can share your dreams with
Share your fears with
Share your loves with

On your voyage to discover your best friend
You may meet many friends along the way
Friends you'll want to sing with
Friends you'll want to eat with
Friends you'll want to dance with
Friends you just want to be with

And then one day
You'll find your best friend of all
You ask me, "How will you know it?"
You ask me, "How will they show it?"

You will feel so comfortable with them
That you'll share a tiny secret
And they will show you beyond a doubt
That they intend to keep it

And the secrets you'll share
Will soon get bigger and deeper
And when they go un-judged
You'll feel support encouragement and love
Then you'll know you've found a keeper

When they pass all these tests, my friends
Then you may have just found your 'Best of Friends'
Oh, by the way, friendships like this...never have to end!

Let 'em Fly

The masses should learn not to keep compliments
And affection locked up inside
Let us release all those winks, that sweet-talk
And the thousand little smiles and let 'em fly!

And keep the ones you love close by
For life can be a wild ride
So, convince the people you love
To hold their heads up high

Allow them to see the upside
Inspire them to try the untried
And within their own skin, take pride

For you just may be their angelic guide
Who can provide them the courage
To cross their personal great divide

Living The Top 10

Of all the days and days that we get to live
We somehow can't remember them all

So, to make space for the new days
That will come with precision
We have to choose the days to remember
Yes, WE have to make that decision

If there's only room for so many
And if you have to erase any...

Let's;
Get rid of the bad ones
And delete the sad ones

The Great ones we'll keep
The Awesome ones we'll repeat

The 'mweh' days, the dreary days
And the 'just OK' days... they gotta go!
So, the space where we keep the Incredible days can grow

Let's Live and Enjoy and Expand
The boundaries of our own reality each day
And Dream BIG, while the impossibilities fade away...

And for the best days we ever lived
Well, let's keep them somewhere really smart
The TOP 10 best days of our life
Go into a Secret High-Security Special place
Tucked deep within our heart

Sailing

There's a funny thing about sailing

Everyone's perceptions are way off

My mom thinks I'm surfing my sailboat down giant tidal waves

My love thinks I'm sailing with 6 bikini babes

My buddies think I'm sailing with six packs of cold beer

The kids think the ol' guy, shows no signs of fear

What really happens when I sail, makes me so uptight!

Most of the time, I'm just trying to keep the boat upright

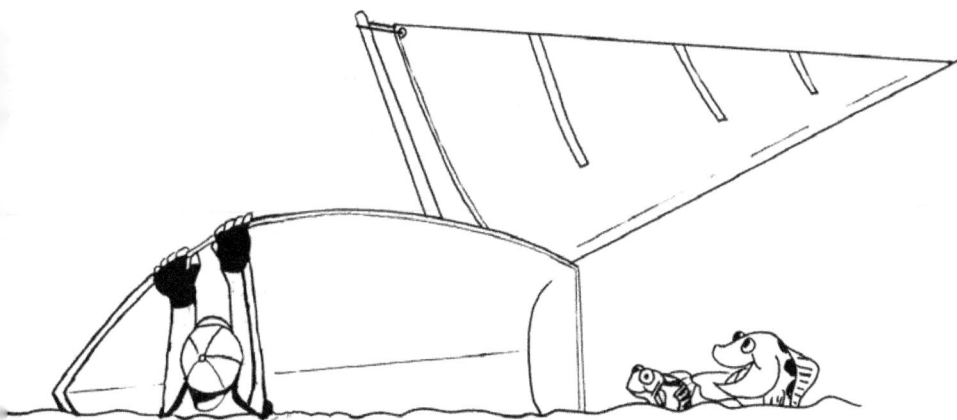

Multi   Tasking

Multi is you more one at time.
When Multi you to more less
However, may better focus one at time,
you being inefficient all jobs are doing.
may faster Multi however, just be and bit

So, time are the reading book talking the
put all and on the paperwork.

Tasking when do than thing a
you Task hope accomplish in time.
it be to on thing a or risk extremely
at the you simultaneously
It be to Task, it may ineffective a
sloppy.
next you on toilet a while on phone
it down concentrate finishing required

*To enjoy this poem,
Here's a hint you should be heeding:
Alternate every word on each side of the page when reading,
or an aspirin you'll soon to be needing!

28

Where To Start?

Whenever I had a new task
And I didn't know when, where, how or why to begin
Dad always gave me the same advice
It was direct, practical and truly concise

He'd look me straight in the eye and say;

"SON"

     "Just Start

           And

             Keep going

                 Until you're...

                     DONE!"

No matter what the endeavor
This advice will work forever!

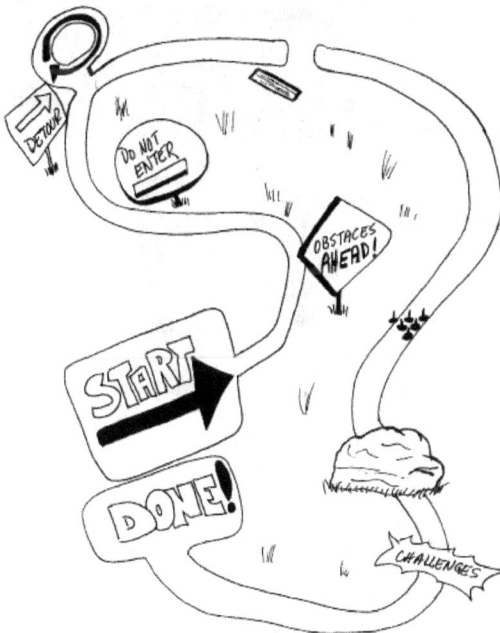

Man vs. Woman

The difference between women and men, is quite easy to spot
If you actually give a squat
Just observe them as they shop
Women buy tissues a lot (a lot, a lot!)
And men just do not

Shapes And Sizes

Did you ever notice when you are at the beach
All the human shapes and sizes?
Yes, God definitely has a sense of humor
He is full of many surprises

Some people are apple shaped
Some people are shaped like a pear
And some have an hourglass design
And some are all covered in hair

Some are long and lanky
And some are as fit as can be
Some have necks like toothpicks
And others, like the trunk of a tree

There are fat people with skinny ankles
And skinny people with fat ones
There are those that weigh in light as a feather
And others you measure by tons

There tall ones, and small ones
Brown ones, and here's a yellow
Pink ones, and spotted ones
And over there is a purple fellow

Why are all people so differently shaped?

Well, one thing is for sure:
There are people shaped like everything under the sun
And it's good that there are lots to choose from
That way there's someone for everyone

31

Hey U!

Universe, help me choose the right path
Please, continue to be my guide
Challenge me to review the options
Allow me the time to truly decide

I understand that Life is not always clear
And that Life may not always seem kind
And I understand, my true calling is out there somewhere
And I know it's up to me to find

I've examined my heart in detail
And I've tested my brain at length
It appears that the road ahead maybe a tricky one
And I need to gather up all my strength

When I listen to you, Universe
When I add up all the signs
I start to see a sketch of your intentions
And that together we are painting a grand design

I appreciate all the signals that you send
About a million little ways each day
They are pointing me in the right direction
They are showing me the way

I don't have all the answers yet
All the stitches are not yet sewn
What I do see is the canvas of something big
And what is to come is more exciting
Than anything I've ever known

Often I look in the mirror and see my reflection
My eyes reveal precisely what can be mine
I see my soul slowly polishing a diamond
Wiping off all the imperfections, allowing it to shine

An individual's journey should be an Awesome one
It should be a voyage of discovery and wonder
It's time to go running in the rain
Dodging the lightning, ignoring the thunder

I do appreciate all your help
And I want you to know that I'm committed
To stripping away the layers of rock
To realize the vein of gold you've permitted

In the end, it's a pretty simple deal
There's really nothing to it
All I have to do is find the one thing
That fills my heart with joy
And DO IT!

The McGee Three

Mrs. McGee was concerned that her boys of three
Were growing up too fast
And that their innocence would not much longer last

Mr. McGee assured Mrs. McGee
That her little boys of three
Were still sweet little boys and undoubtedly he knows it
So, Mr. McGee told Mrs. McGee
"I have the perfect test that will show it"

So, Mr. McGee shouted to his boys of three
"Boys! Where are your BALLS at?!"
As they were playing in the yard by the gumbo-limo tree

A 'not so charming' answer Mrs. McGee did assume
However, the McGee three shouted back quite harmlessly
"Our balls are in the toy room!"

"You see Mrs. McGee?" said Mr. McGee very confidently
"Your boys of three are still as innocent as can be!"

Sweaty Betty

My friend Sweaty Betty wouldn't be nearly so sweaty
If she would take off that old woolen sweater
She told me once she'd LOVE to take it off
Her parents just simply won't let her

That Guy

Oh no!
Here comes that guy
Walking down the street
If I don't turn, we're gonna have to meet

He's walking straight at me
He's a fast-walker!
I don't want to talk to him
He's such a close-talker!

Oh man!
I just wanna get my things together
And get on my way
I don't want to waste my time
Talking to him all day

Ahhh! Now it's too late
We're gonna have to talk
Keep it light ...
I'll just get up and start to walk

Yes, I'll just say "Hi"
And walk on by...

Here he comes
I'll just say "HI" and be on my way
Here it goes:
"Hi!, What's up?"… What did I just say?!

Now he's starting to tell me
All the things in his life
His work, his family
His hobbies, his dreams
His favorite books, movies
And flavors of ice cream

Oh! This has been long...
And now I sense it's coming to a close!
Why I asked him "What's up?", I'll just never know

Ok, finally, we are saying goodbye
He's actually a pretty nice guy
I kind of actually enjoyed the chat
Funny how things work out like that

I'm glad we wound up playing that silly little game
I like my old pal.............?
Shoot! I forgot his name!

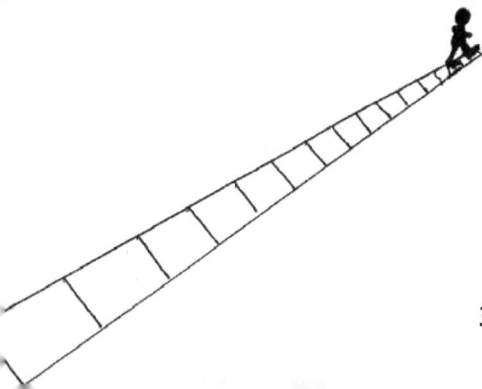

The Creatures Of Habit

The Creatures of Habit
They sneak in at night
They take away your vision
While they hide in plain sight

The Creatures of Habit
Seek to diminish your life
When you try to eliminate them
They will put up a fight

The Creatures of Habit
They make no pretenses
It's best to stay on the offensive
For they aim to weaken your senses

The Creatures of Habit
They travel in packs
The simple trick to beating them
Is to push back their attacks

The Creatures of Habit
Have to be challenged right away
Because if they get a hold of you
You'll be cursed to doing the same things,
In the same way,
Day after Day after Day....

Rebuilding

When you have somehow fallen deep in pain
And you are dreading each hourly strain
It may be natural that your confidence
May start to seriously wane

Remember, to make time to listen to your body
And listen to your soul
They will tell you everything you need to know
To once again be healthy and whole

And when you are caught up in your darkest hour
When you are not living at your highest power
Stop to visualize the rebuilding of your personal tower

Start at the foundation and work your way higher
Building yourself back brick by brick
Demanding to rest before you tire
Cementing strong unions and pausing to rekindle your fire

You will find yourself better than that you were before
And able to journey longer
Look at your reflection now my friend,
Better, Wiser and Stronger!

Sushi Rules

When you are eating SUSHI with your Best-Friend
(Girl or Boy),
I recommend you don't mix up the little cups
(of the SAKI and the SOY)

On Guard

I heard you got some information today
That was "less than good" let's just say

So:

Take a deep breath, (that's step one)
And then go ahead and take another one

Then make sure the information is true
(That's the second thing to do)

If it's true, remember this verse
'Make sure YOU don't make it worse'

Think straight, think clear (do it somehow)
And stay far away from fear (for now)

In every situation, a hero needs to arrive (so YOU do it)
Be the person that helps
Everyone else to continue through it

So, for now, you be the caretaker of Universal courage
(Yes, it's up to you to mind it)
The others may desperately need to borrow some strength
So it's up to you to find it!

Tryit Diet

I heard you are starting
Another strict weight loss diet
Well, here's one piece of advice
(It's confidential, so let's keep it quiet)

Last night, you had two orders of Mac'n'cheese
With a side order of double cheeseburger!
You ate it all; I didn't think you'd go through with it!
Your weight issue...That may have something to do with it

So, if you want to keep fit
Here's a good diet:
Eat good foods and be active
(Go ahead and try it)

Secret Ingredient

When you are making an Apology
Leave out the excuses (they can taste bitterly)
Fill it full of Sweet Sincerity

It will come out just right
And go down real easy

B U!

Zipper is a Penguin
That doesn't like swimming in cold water
Yes, Zipper is a rare bird
Who doesn't live where he oughter

Zipper doesn't play by the rules,
He lives his life how and where he likes
No snow, no minus degrees, no frost and no ice

So, If you need inspiration to change your life,
Zipper is your man!
Oh, and as for Global Warming?
Zipper is a Big Fan!

3 States Of Growth

1. Doing what you do

2. Learning something new

3. Taking time to renew

Watch Out For 'Kerfluffles'!

I woke up this morning,
And I was calm as can be
I strode to the kitchen
And carefully poured myself some green tea

Then I gently opened the newspaper
And turned to page 43
For it was the horoscope I was wanting to see

I routinely found my zodiac sign and I proceeded to read:
"Watch out for 'Kerfluffles'"
Now, what does that mean?!
What are 'Kerfluffles!'?

This really worried me!
What can they be?
Are they small like a mouse?
Or big like a tree?

Can they Bite, Fly or Run?
Can they Growl, Swim and Breed?
Are they Poisonous? Ravenous?
Are they prone to STAMPEDE?
I was lacking information,
I was in trouble guaranteed!

So, I warned all my friends, neighbors and family
"Watch out for 'Kerfluffles!!'" just as fast as could be!

Then I quickly informed the news services,
The police, then the Army and the Navy!
It seemed no one knew anything about 'Kerfluffles!!!',
So then we all agreed

We would double and triple fortify our watch,
We would form a nationwide decree
To "WATCH OUT FOR 'KERFLUFFLES"!!!!',
So everyone should take heed!

We could not have the public Panic,
With Ballyhoo, Blather and Bobbery!

We have to contain large Disturbances,
Foofaraws, Hullabaloos and Corroborees!

We just can't have Helter-Skelter,
Commotion, nor mass Shindy!!!
It'S UP TO US TO STOP WIDE-SPREAD PANDEMONIUM,
WILLIWAW, RUCKUS, AND CACOPHONY!!!!

Will you join us! Will you help?
I'm on my knees to you pleading!:
WATCH OUT FOR 'KERFLUFFLES'!!!!!
It's YOUR help we are needing!

Sweet Little Maria

Today, Sweet little Maria fell down the stairs!
From what we heard...it was all arms legs and hairs!

She was wearing new shoes and they didn't fit just right…
She lost her footing and fell down two flights!
Oh, what a sight!

The neighbors heard her scream from 3 miles away!
Her dogs and cats watched in horror
Without a word to say!

When she stopped falling...
And God's name she stopped calling...

She gathered her wits, and straightened her dress…
And fixed herself, so she wouldn't look a mess.

Then she took a deep breath,
OK...everything is all right!
Then she missed another step!
And she fell down the next flight!

When Maria eventually stopped tumbling to the ground…
Luckily nothing was broken, no bruises could be found!

We were all so relieved to hear
There was no damage to her physique…
And Maria was glad that
She only has to wear these shoes TWO TIMES a week!

Busy Busy!

I'm so busy!

The emails

The texts

The posts

The blogs

The notes

The blurbs

The shows

The logs

The sites

The greetings

The calls

The meetings!

I'm so busy...Am I the only one?
I'm just so busy ....getting nothing done!

"Dogs Are Smarter Than People"

"Dogs are SMARTER than people"
There, I said it!
"Dogs are smarter than PEOPLE"
That's right, I wrote it down and YOU read it

My developed hypothesis is simple
Allow me to explain it to you:
"Dogs ARE smarter than people"
I will now explain why my theory is true

Admittedly, my dog may not be the
'Brightest pup at the dog show'
That being said,
He can speak at least 2 languages that I know

Besides naturally knowing how to speak to other dogs
He obviously knows 'people talk'
He comprehends the words I say to him like:
"Treat", "fetch", "roll over" and "let's take a walk"

And he follows these commands precisely, everyday
Therefore, he must understand the 'people words' that I say

So, if dogs can learn 'people talk'
Then I ask you 'Why?'
Why can't people learn 'dog talk'?
No matter how hard we try?

My dog says "Bark!", "Yap Yap!", "Arf!"
"Bow Wow!", "Grrrrr.." and "whinnnne"
I just don't understand any of it!
And I'm hearing him just fine!

And I don't know anyone who ever did, or currently does
So, it's logical to conclude then
That "dogs are smarter" than the rest of us

Besides that, all my dog does all day
Is lie around in the sun and play
No stress, no work, no troubles, no care
And that is more proof that dogs
Are among the most intelligent life found anywhere

To conclude, "Dogs are SMARTER than people"
Because they communicate to anyone anywhere
And lead their lives without fuss
Maybe that is something we should all learn
A lesson from the dogs…
To the rest of us

The Comeback!

I'm expecting a big comeback from you!
And I'm expecting you to start really soon!

I'm sorry if it seems selfish,
I kinda know it is, that's true
I just need you to see yourself,
The way that I see you

The strongest person I ever knew
My rock, my pillar, the idol who stood by me as I grew

Tell me again your funny stories, like only you can do 'em
Tell me again about your biggest adventures,
I always love to listen to 'em

Please let's sing together some of our favorite songs
You start singing, and I'll follow along

I see you in agony, I know it must hurt
Seeing you in pain is making my heart start to burst

I'm expecting a big comeback from you,
Let's start right now!
You can do it, I believe in you, I trust you!
You showed me how!

Hopin' Ocean

I'm scared
Scared of this vast open ocean that's in front of me
Scared of what I cannot see
I'm scared of the potential, and what's to be

I'm scared
Scared that I don't have all the answers
Scared I don't have 100 percent certainty
Scared of being in too deep and over my head for this swim
I'm scared of not being strong enough to win

However, I do have a genuine faith
And I do feel surrounded in love
And I do have an immense trust in the signs sent to me
From the Universe above

And with that, I believe I can beat this ocean
That I now see so clearly
All it will take is an Awesome leap of faith!
Perhaps you will join me?
I can swim this ocean you know!
I believe I can beat it, positively!

Because no matter how rough the seas get,
The secret to winning:
Is to just keep swimming!

So Happy!

You make me so Happy! I'm filled up like a balloon
I'm so full of Happy; I can't fit inside the room!

I have to leave the inside and go outside to get air!
I feel like taking a Happy flight to I-don't-care-where!

I'm drifting higher and higher into deep outer space
With the world's Happiest smile
Written right across my face

I'm feeling so blessed, so euphoric and ever so bright
So pleased, so fortunate and so full of delight!

I feel like singing and flying and jumping with pleasure
Having you in my life is like holding a treasure!

Encouragement

Wow, You look so Young and so Cute!
When you are cooking and
Cleaning around the house
There's not a beauty that can top you!
Please continue, Don't let me stop you!

Wow! You look so Strong and so Handsome!
When you are fixing things around the house
There's not a manlier man
That can top you!
Please continue,
Don't let me stop you!

One More Day

Is it that time my Friend?
You've clearly signaled to me it's your time
It's your life, your planning, so allow me to align mine

Lately, there seems to be no easy rest for you
You've always known, how to manage yourself
So whatever is best for you...

I guess you figured your time is now gone
And it's time for you to move on
To be once again young and strong

It's time to chase cats again
And to run at full speed
Eat all the things you really love
And pee on whatever you please

You been a loyal and a true friend
And you've given us your best 'till the end
You've aged with dignity and grace
Although lately the smile's been gone from your face

I know now what the lack of tail wagging
These past few weeks meant
And I know now for what you have,
There is no treatment

And there's nothing more I can say
You've been the best dog I've ever known
A perfect companion in every way
Just stay with me one more day

Yes, we'll share one more Best Day
Eating raw meat, bacon and cheese
I'll open the refrigerator
And you can choose whatever you please

We'll go for one last swim
Don't worry I'll hold you as we go in
One last ride in the car
It's just around the block, not very far

Try to stick your nose in the air
And feel the wind on your snout
And give a bark at whoever you like
These things are what living is all about

Let us prepare for a Goodbye my Friend
Today, you should plan yourself a rest day
And I'll start working on tomorrow
And together we will share one more Best Day.

So, what do you say,
One more Best Day?

When The Smoke Clears

"You are so genuinely beautiful;

You make my eyes almost blind!"

"What, you didn't hear me?

You want to borrow a cigarette lighter?

Hmmm, never mind!"

The Hunter

Mr. I.C. Ashot is a hunter,
That much we know is true
It is the one thing
He seemed perfectly cut out to do

He hunted animals by looking for clues
In forests, in mountains and in jungles too

He shot them,
Then hung them on his walls
When he was through

It may seem cruel,
It may be hard to construe

Just know this...
Mr. I.C. Ashot only shoots animals with cameras,
Whew!

The Middle

Please, meet me in the middle on this
I assure you, my intentions are not amiss

Let's meet in the middle on this issue
So, neither one of us will need a tissue

Let's meet in the middle, so it's fair for all
There's no challenge too big, nor one too small

Let's meet in the middle, it won't take much work
And neither one of us will feel the jerk

Let's meet in the middle on this deal
And our friendship we shall seal

We can definitely find a way
When we meet in the middle today!

Welcome to the **Middle** Pop. 2 (me and you)

Victory

Before every Great Victory there lies a field
Full of beaten challenges
And the remnants of accomplished tasks

While holding the laurels of triumph
Make the time to recognize the moment
Appreciate those that helped you succeed
And record the lessons learned

Then start your plans to create your next masterwork!

The Audience

In the shower: I sing with Power!

In the Car: I am a SuperStar!

Alone at my Desk: I am the Best!

Riding my Bike: Hand me the Mic!

The words I know, the songs they flow

I sing with Passion and... you want me to what?

Come sing aloud? In front of a crowd?

In front of friends and family?

Display my skills? And bare my soul?

For everyone to see?

Hmmmmmmmmm,

Let me think about how brave I want to be...

Auntie Advice

My Aunt always said one thing

"I have some advice for you
When someone wants to give you things
If it's for free, take two!"

Just remember to thank people kindly and be elated
Because free gifts are so seldom appreciated

Bath Time

I took a bath with a Mermaid today...

What an adventure that turned out to be!

I'm going to do anything to keep her happy...

So, she doesn't return to the sea!

Fountain Of Trust

Trust is a beautiful water fountain
Flowing from a source of promises

Some vows spring small like a water trickle
And some commitments run oceans deep

Just remember, the only promises that really matter
Are the ones that we truly keep

Hammer Time?

Live your life with Spirit
And give everyday your Best
And when the 'Man with the Hammer' comes
Tell him you're NOT ready to Rest

Crush 'em

The scariest Monsters we will ever face in our lives
Are all born from the tiniest little egg of self-doubt

Crush those little creatures when they are small,
And they can't bother you at all!

The Journey

Well, hello my friend!
Do you have a moment with me to spend?
Please allow me to share a story with you;
I'm hoping it will have a happy end:)

You see, a long time ago, I made a journey to see the Guru
Who lives at the top of Mt. LISTINTAWUTATELYU
I needed to find out 'Life's Greatest Truth'

I was given a very detailed map with instructions
On some enjoyable stops to make
And some peaceful breaks to take
And what kind of friends to make

There were notes on the map saying
"You must find happiness every single day"
And *"Your journey will take many years,*
So, you better start today!"
I decided this will take much too long,
So, I went my own way

I skipped the stops I was supposed to make
I worked through the breaks I was told to take
I never bothered with friends I needed to make

I reached the top of the mountain in record time
And I was feeling exhausted from the pace of my climb
Now "Life's Greatest Truth" would be mine to find!

I found the Guru,
He was sitting alone in the sun basking
The Guru looked me up and down
As I stood before him sweating and gasping
And these questions he began asking:
"Did you find enjoyment
In the stops you were supposed to make?"
"Did you enjoy the peacefulness
In the breaks you were requested to take?"
"Did you share love with the friends you needed to make?"

I told him I didn't take the time
Because I wanted to get to the top faster
He looked me right in the eye and told me
"That decision was a disaster!"
And *"You have failed to find what you have sought after"*

So, he sent me back down the mountain,
And here is where I've been living
And here is some advice for you I need to be giving:

Enjoy every stop you choose to make
(and make many)
Fill your time with peaceful breaks to take
(and take plenty)
Share love with friends you are fortunate to make
(enemies..don't make any)

So, that's my story my friend,
I hope it's been worth your time
And if one day you meet the Guru,
Please tell him from me
"Thank You, I'm doing just fine!"

Forgiveness

If you really want a heart that beats strong and true
Forgive someone fully for what they may have done to you

And if, by chance, they do the same thing to you once more
Forgive them again, just like you did before

See, you can't make the future
And you can't change the past
What you can do is build love on a foundation of trust
That can last & last & last

Forgive To Forget

Forgive To Forget

I can forgive you
And I can forget, my friend
Just don't keep "reminding" me
By doing it again and again...

Race Yourself Or Brace Yourself

When you find yourself in a conversation one of these days
And the person you are talking to begins to say
The following phrase:

I don't mean to criticize...
Or

Don't take this the wrong way...
Or

No offense...
Or

I don't mean any harm...

Please listen; those words should sound an alarm!

Immediately, get up and run!
What's coming next will be no fun!

The next words spoken will be rough and tough
And may be bringing some stinging

So, RUN! Don't walk!
Do what you can do get out of that talk!

Those warm-up words are just a sugary start
To set a sweet pace

What's coming next is that person
Sticking their big ol' "BUT" right in your face

Right The Wrong

If you are wrong
You are wrong
So, say you are sorry
And don't take too long

If you are wrong
You are wrong
Make no excuses
Don't sing a big song

If you are wrong, there's not much more to say
So, at least be wrong in the right-est of ways

The Eye-Witness

I wanted to see a change…
So, I sat in front of a mirror for 50 years…
And I stared at myself from my toes to my ears

50 long years to see what time would bring
50 years! And I never noticed a thing!

The Search

The search is on
For what you are lacking
Keep digging until you find it
Never stop attacking

The search is on
For what's driving your mind
Keep looking and the hints will appear
Note the clues down, don't leave them behind

The search is on
For the piece you are needing
Stay calm, Don't panic
And you can start completing

The picture soon will be clear
The puzzle surely will be whole
And you can the see the full idea
And that will ignite the fire in your soul

Take It All The Way

You can pretend to be who you are not
Or you can live out who you are

One path will get you nowhere fast
And the other route will take you soooooo far!

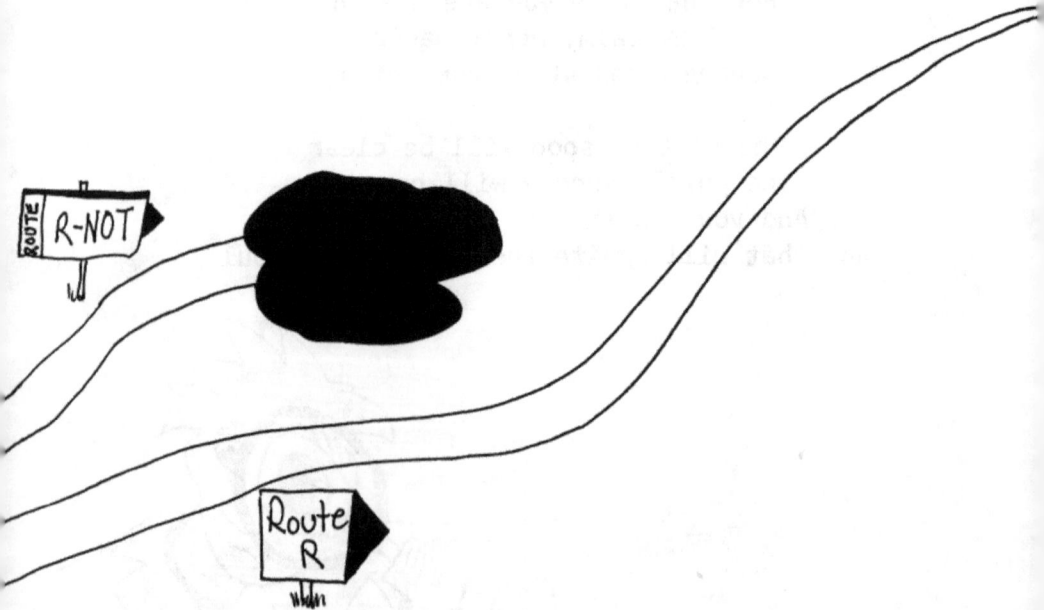

ROUTE R-NOT

Route
R

Taxi?

Taxi? Taxi?
Mister...Taxi?
"No"
Mister... Taxi, Taxi?
"No, No"
Mister... Taxi, Taxi, Taxi?
"No, No, No!"

What do the taxi drivers know that I don't?
I want them to leave me alone, they just won't!

100 times they ask
200 times I deny
In spite of that, they try and try and...

Actually, I really do need a taxi now, "Goodbye!"

About the Author

J. Leone is the author-artist of the 3 part series Living, Laughing and Loving, Poems for an Awesome! Life.

He is a private business owner, a writer of songs and available for public speaking.

He can be spotted in Awesome! places like New York City; Princeton, NJ; Miami, FL; Amsterdam, The Netherlands and on the beautiful Caribbean island of St. Maarten

GreenSpring
greenspringnv@gmail.com

www.ingramcontent.com/pod-product-compliance
Lightning Source LLC
Chambersburg PA
CBHW071838020426
42331CB00007B/1777